F O R R E S T   W I L S O N

What It Feels Like To Be A Building

Landmark Reprint Series

The Preservation Press

National Trust
for Historic Preservation

The Preservation Press
National Trust for Historic Preservation
1785 Massachusetts Avenue, N.W.
Washington, D.C. 20036

The National Trust for Historic Preservation is the only private, nonprofit organization chartered by Congress to encourage public participation in the preservation of sites, buildings and objects significant in American history and culture. Support is provided by membership dues, endowment funds, contributions and grants from federal agencies, including the U.S. Department of the Interior, under provisions of the National Historic Preservation Act of 1966. The opinions expressed herein do not necessarily reflect the views or policies of the Interior Department. For information about membership in the National Trust, write to the above address.

Library of Congress Cataloging in Publication Data

Wilson, Forrest, 1918–
    What it feels like to be a building.

    (Landmark reprint series)
    Summary: Explains how different parts of a building, such as columns, walls, beams, buttresses, rods and cables, function to support great weight and stress.
    1. Structural engineering — Juvenile literature.   2. Buildings — Juvenile literature.
[1. Buildings   2. Structural engineering]
I. Title.   II. Series
TA634.W55   1988   690′.21   88-22382
ISBN 0-89133-142-5
ISBN 0-89133-147-6 (pbk.)

Printed in the United States of America

95 94   5 4 3

For my wife and my children, Jonathan, Robert and Paul.
And for my students, who for so many years
have so kindly and graciously allowed me to think
that I was teaching them while they were teaching me.

Building Body Language

Everyone can understand buildings. You feel gravity,
wind, sun and rain. Buildings feel the same stresses
and strains that people do. For this reason
you can put yourself in a building's place.
When you feel what it feels like to be a building,
you can talk to buildings and they will talk to you
in building body language.

Buildings stand up because gravity pulls them down

toward the center of the earth.

Gravity feels like glue.

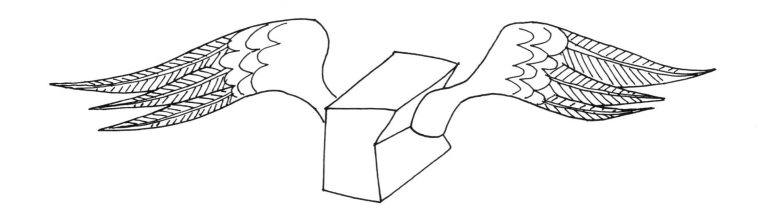

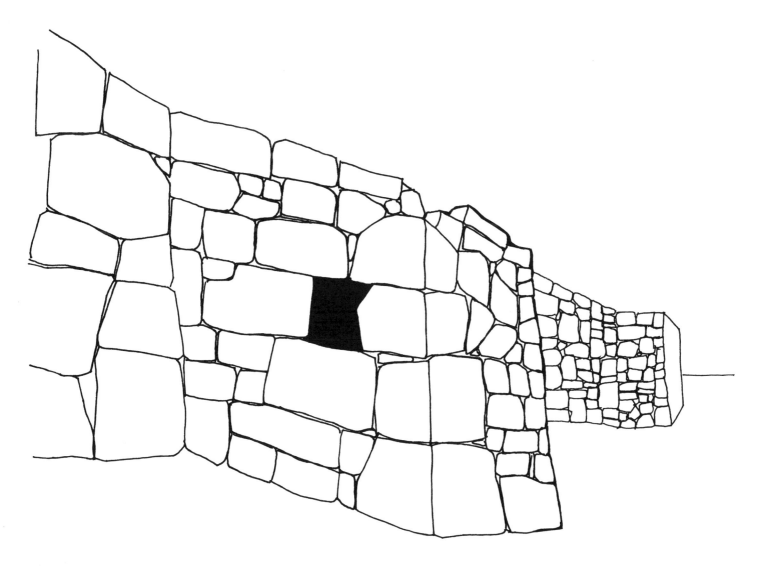

If it did not, stones would fly.

It feels like SQUASH to be a column,
because columns
are squashed between a building and the ground.

Even though a column might be disguised in squiggles,
it still feels squashed.

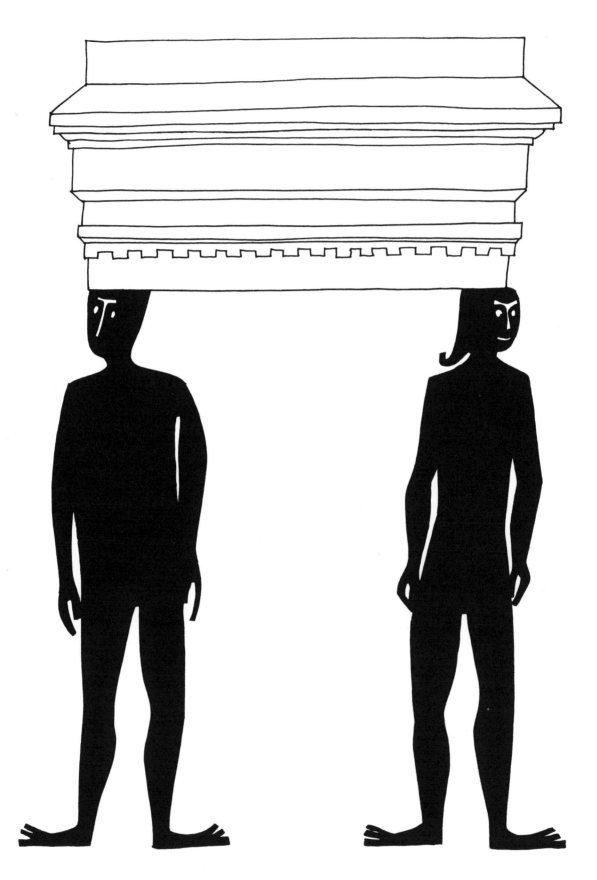

Columns must stand straight up as they push straight down
to carry the weight of a building to the ground.

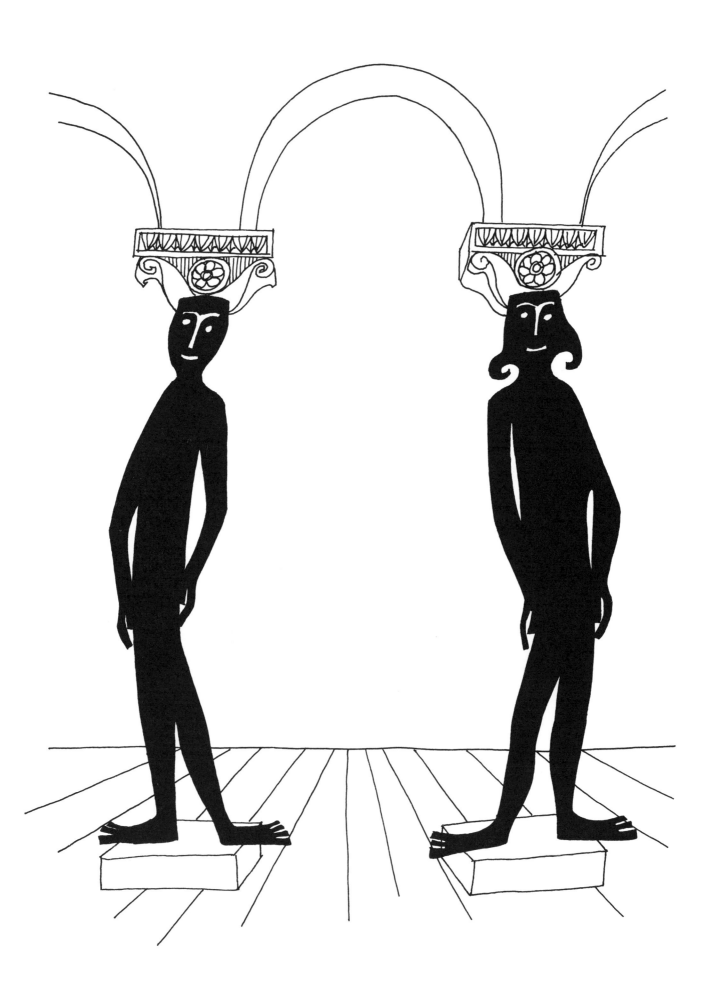

Long thin columns tend to bend,

short to shatter.

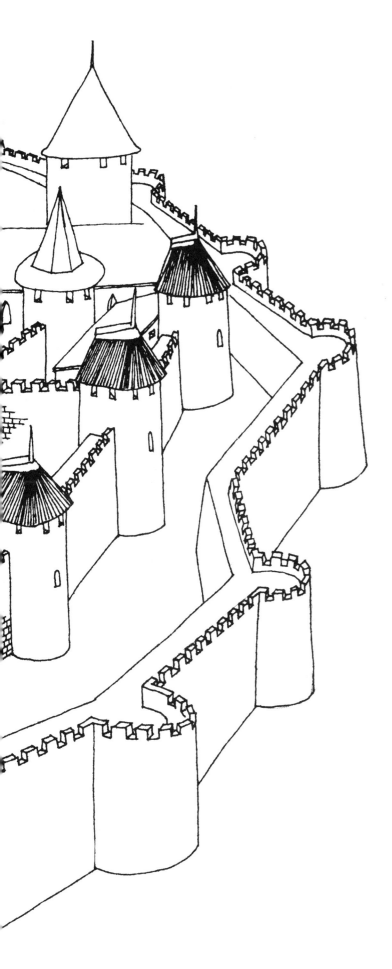

Walls do the same thing that columns do, only more.

It feels like multiple SQUASH to be a wall,
because being wider and longer than a column,
a wall carries more of a building's weight to the ground.

The ground must push up as hard as columns and walls push down,

although sometimes columns and walls push harder.

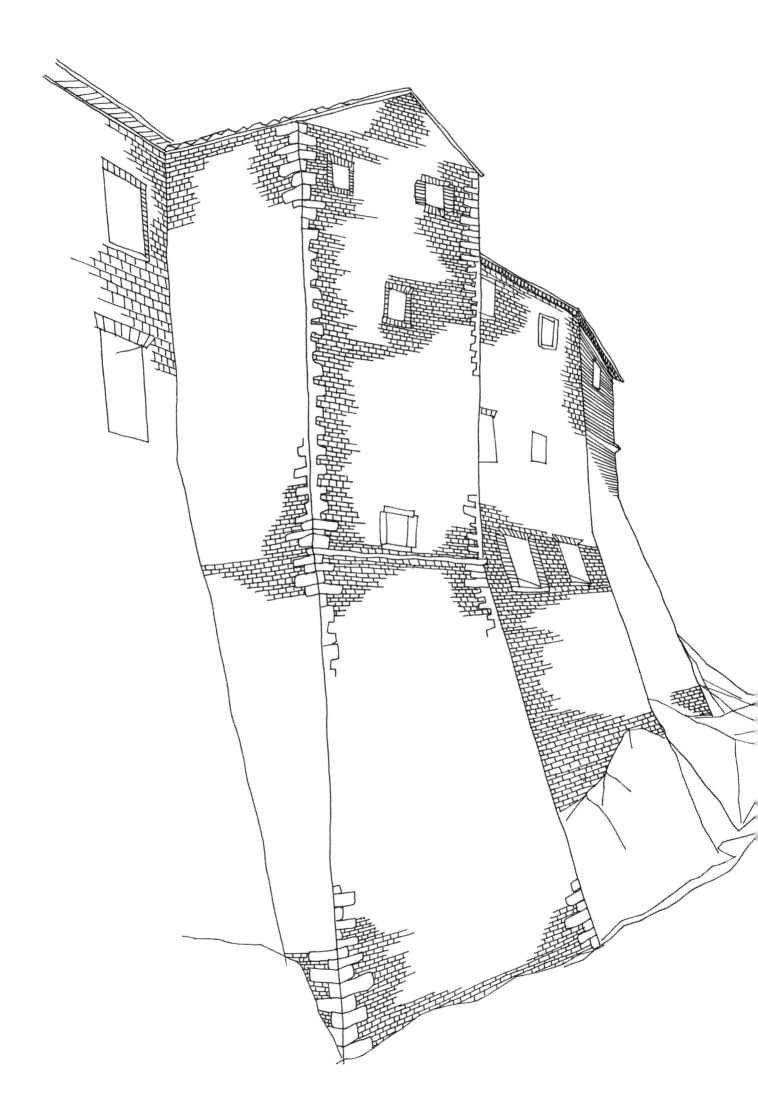

Buildings must get stronger near the bottom,
because the closer they get to the ground,
the more weight they carry over their heads.

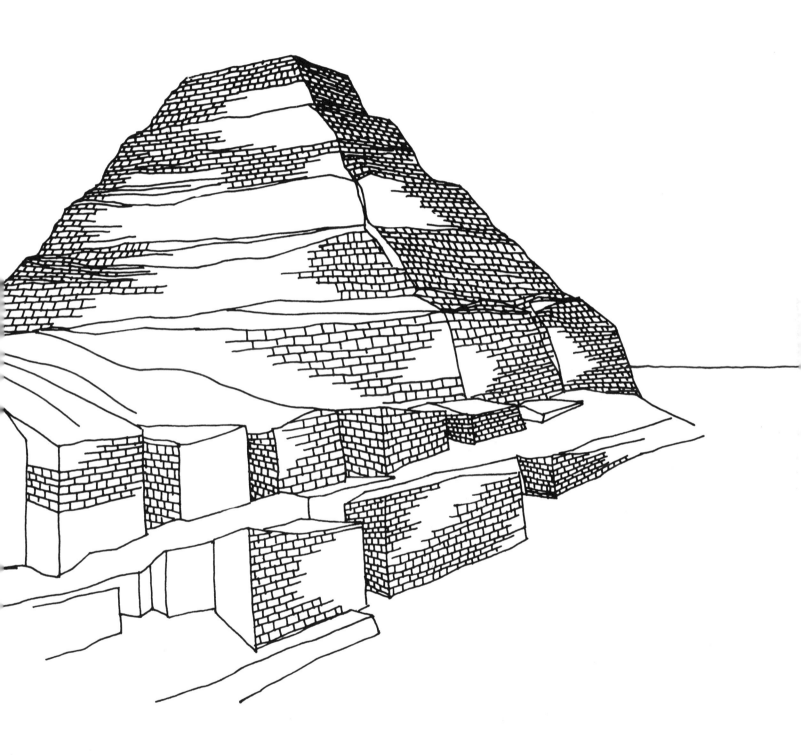

This is why pyramids are wider at the bottom than they are at the top.

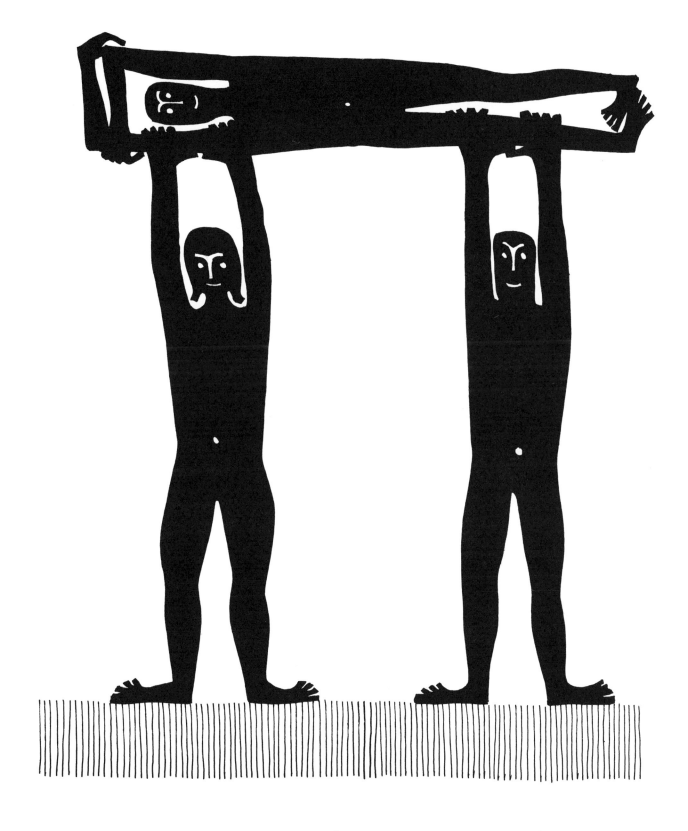

It feels like *BEND* to be a beam, because

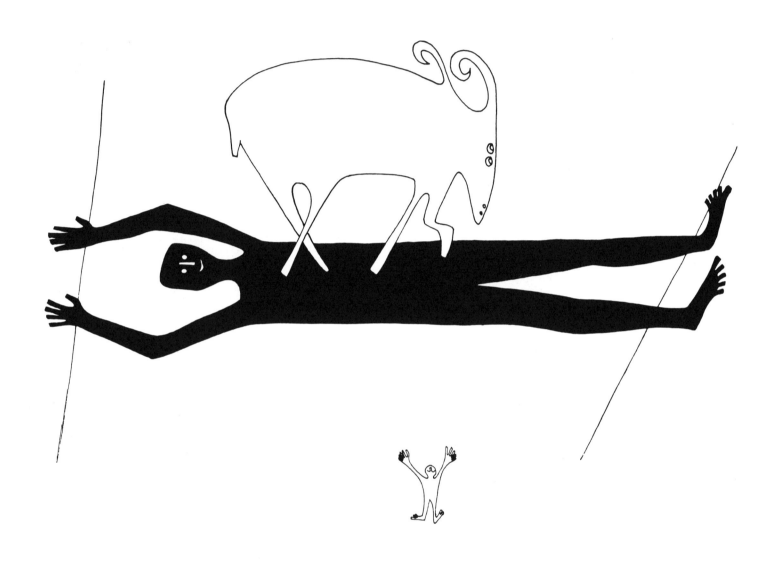

the beam does not, like the column and the wall,
carry weight straight down.
It carries the weight across to its supports.

This makes the top of the beam feel like getting shorter
by pushing together and its bottom feel like
getting longer by pulling apart.

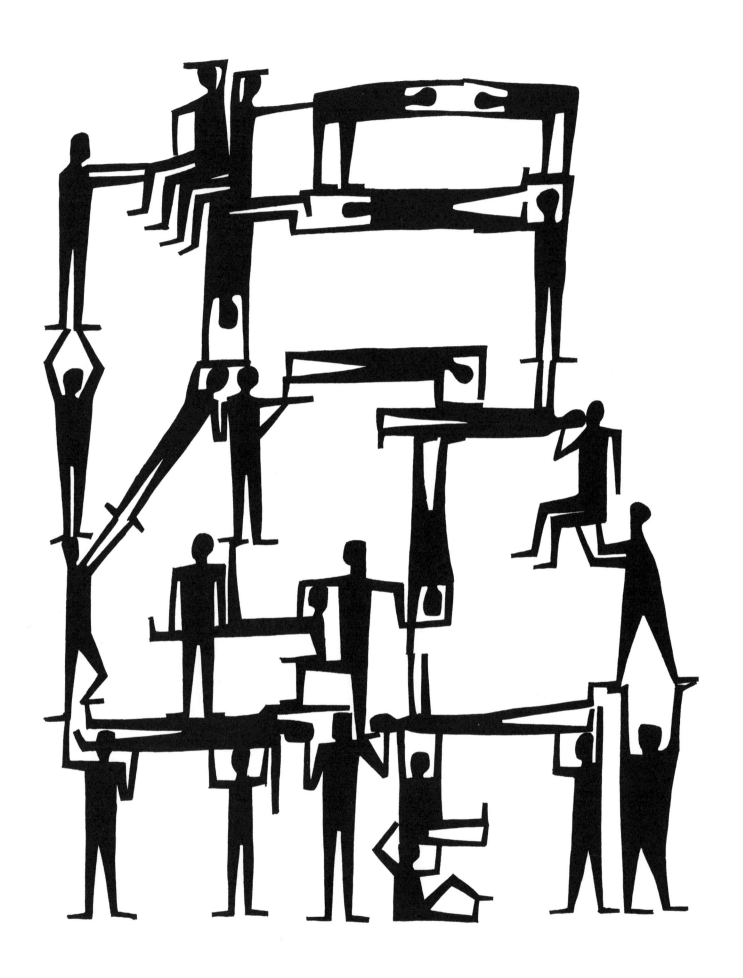

But beams cannot bend too much because they would split in the middle.

This is why roofs supported by beams are flat.

Sometimes beams are inclined to butt,

but they push and pull to stay straight even when placed at an angle.

This is what it feels like to be a house with beams on an angle,

resting on walls that stand straight up as they push straight down.

A Greek temple has the same feeling as a house,
only much more serious. It has very important columns standing up
while pushing straight down, with short, strong, straight beams
between the columns and impressive butting beams over all of this.

If you felt like a Greek temple, you would feel very important,
but you would still feel squashed, bent and inclined to butt.

It feels like DROOP to be a corbel,

because corbels are not very ambitious. They are content

to carry just a little bit of the load at a time.

The word "corbel" comes from the Latin word "corvus"
for raven or crow, which is quite sensible
because crows are corbelled at both ends.

A corbel is dogged.

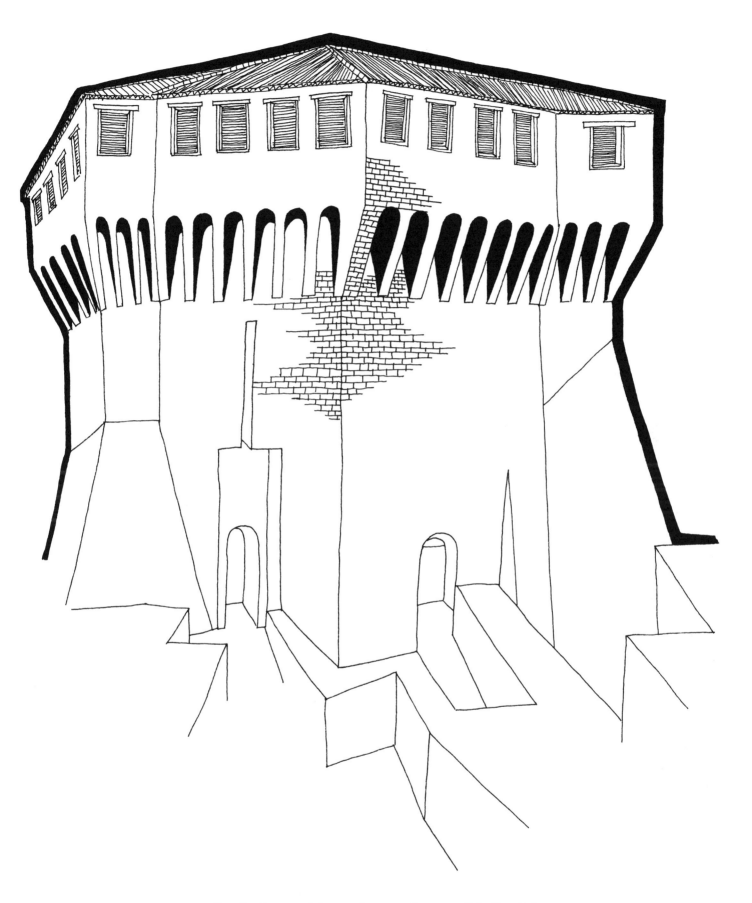

Corbels stubbornly push out, bit by bit,

in little upside-down steps,

as they carry the load back to a building's walls.

It feels like SQUEEZE to be an arch, because an arch
is all squeeze-push with no pull at all.

Rounded forms in buildings show that squeezing arches are at work.

Arches squeeze around these windows in a tower,
which stands straight up while being pulled straight down.

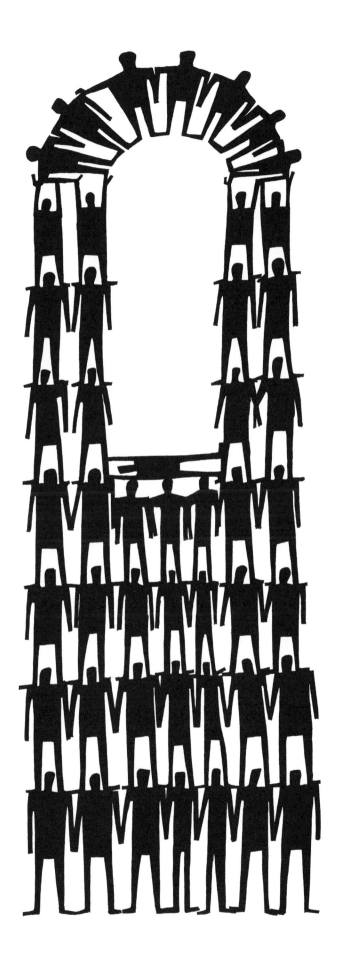

This is how an arched window in a tower feels.

Domes, like a circle of arches,

feel like multiple SQUEEZE because they push in all directions.

Columns nap.

Walls doze.

Corbels drowse.

But the arch never sleeps.

It feels like *BRACE* to be a buttress,

because a buttress supports a building's walls.

A buttress pushes in against a wall at exactly the place

where the wall feels most like pushing out.

This would happen

if buttresses did not push in.

This is a tower of walls and buttresses and butting beams.

Four butting beams
make a pointed tower top,

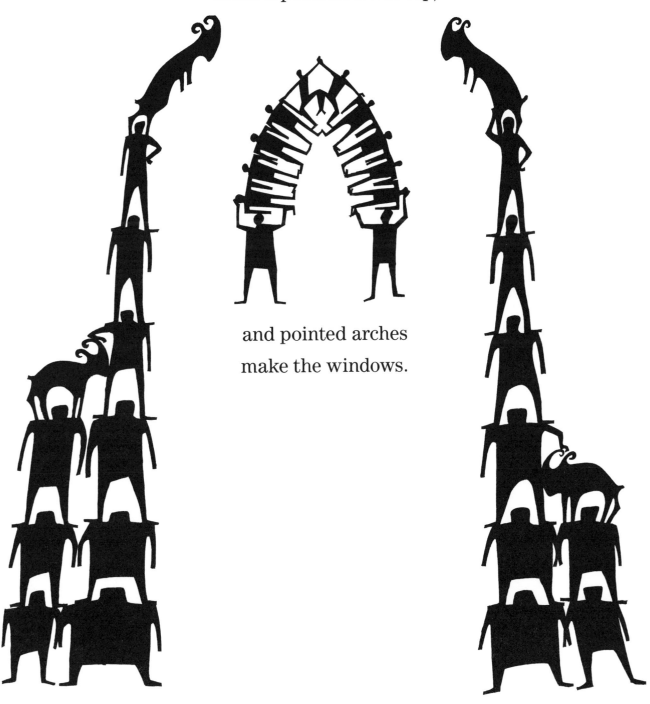

and pointed arches
make the windows.

Buttresses hold up the tower walls.

A flying buttress is the arch's cousin.

It is like half an arch that flies from its support
to brace a wall in the air.

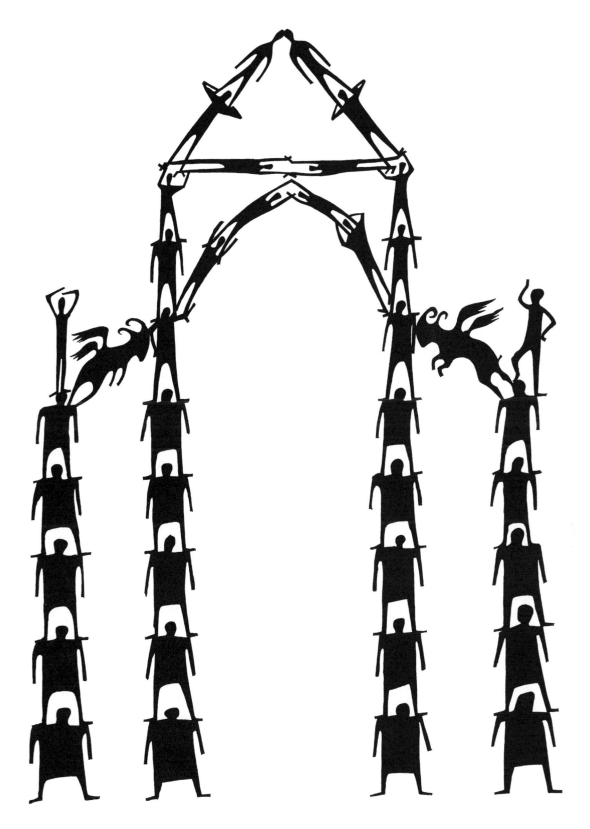

This is how it feels to be a cathedral with walls that stand up
while they push straight down, topped by butting beams that push out
and flying buttresses that take to the air to push them back again.

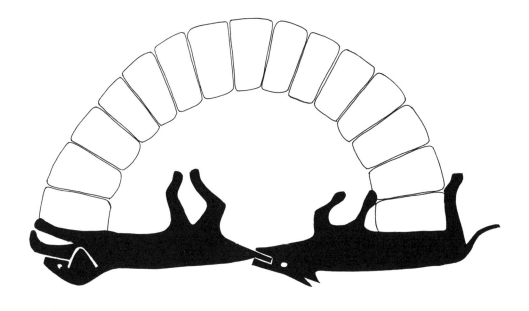

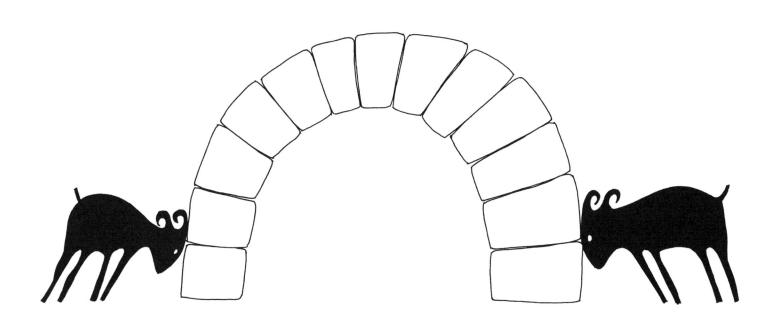

where buttresses would push.

Cables are relaxed when things are slack,

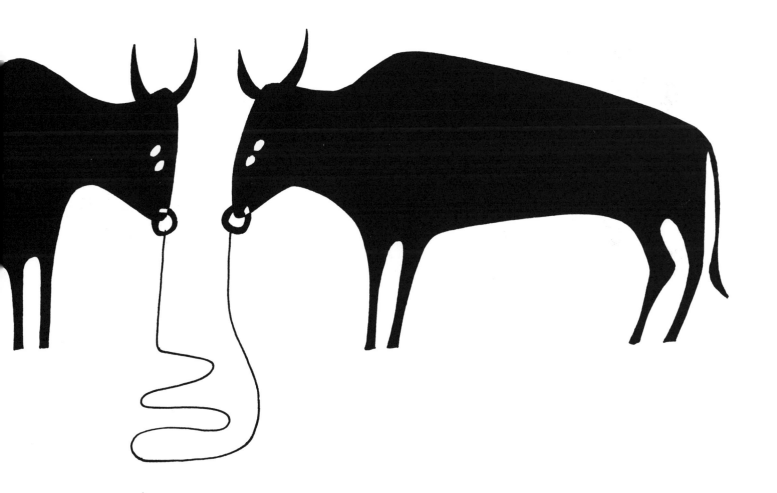

but when you see the pull of tension,

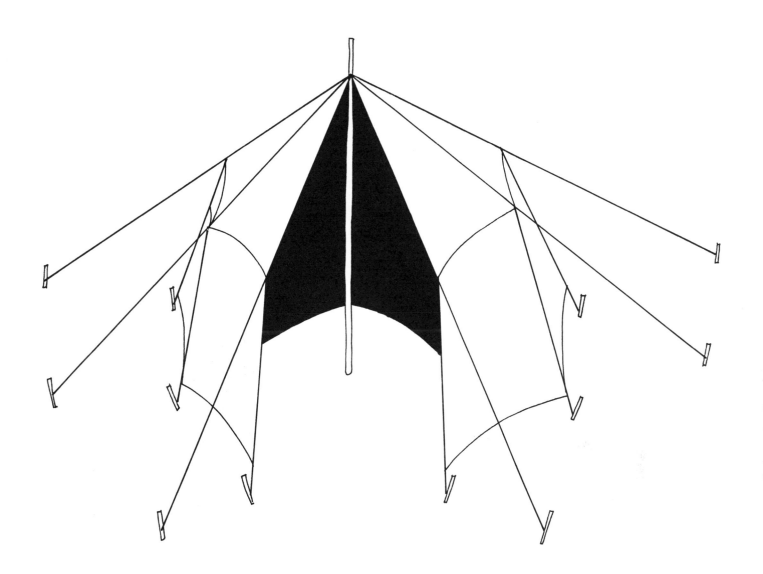

you know that cables are working.

So, *PUSH*

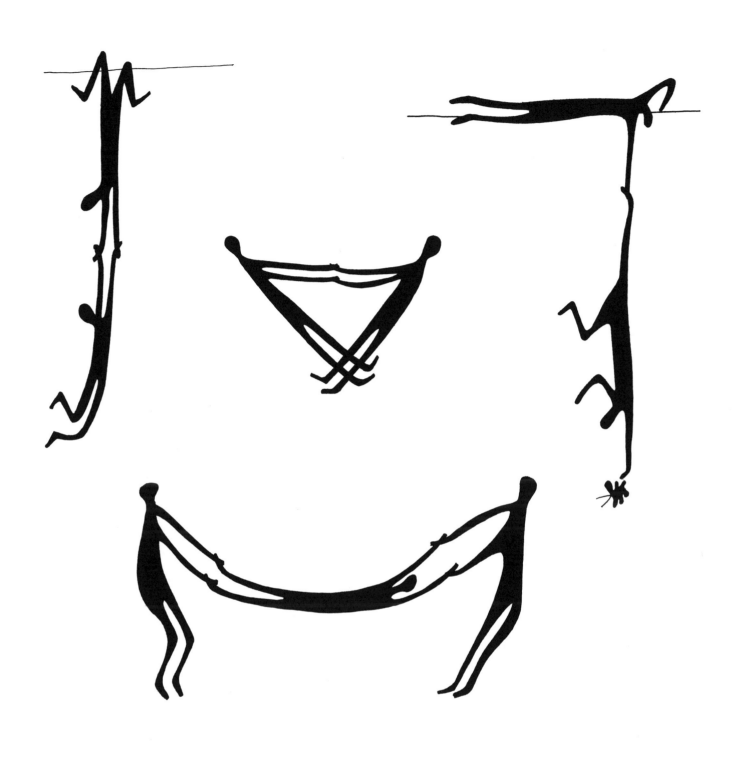

or PUZZ

or

SQUASH

SQUEEZE

DROOP

TUG

BEND

or

BRACE,

that's what it feels like to be a building!

Forrest Wilson

Forrest Wilson earned his carpenter's union card while working his way through the California School of Fine Arts, where he studied architectural sculpture. He has been a ship's carpenter, construction superintendent, professor of architectural design and construction, editor of *Progressive Architecture*, director of the School of Architecture, Design and Planning at Ohio University, associate dean of the School of Engineering and Architecture and chairman of the Department of Architecture at The Catholic University of America. He has written numerous articles and 16 books on architecture, design and building for children and adults, including *Architecture: A Book of Projects for Young Adults* and *City Planning: The Game of Human Settlements*.

Wilson is professor emeritus of The Catholic University, Washington, D.C., visiting professor at The Catholic University and the University of Maryland, and senior editor for technology for *Architecture*, the journal of the American Institute of Architects.